Kindergarten Sight Words Workbook

(Baby Professor Learning Books)

SPEEDY
PUBLISHING

Speedy Publishing LLC
40 E. Main St. #1156
Newark, DE 19711
www.speedypublishing.com

an

\ən, (ˈ)an\

a a a a a

That is an elephant.

and

\ən(d), (ˈ)an(d)\

and and and and

John and Ryan are boys.

am

\ˈā-ˌem\

am am am am

I am a kid.

are

\ˈer, ˈär\

are are are are

They are playing golf.

at

\ət, ˈat\

at at at at

Look at you!

can

\kən, ˈkan also ˈken; dial ˈkin\

can can can can

She can sing.

do

\ˈdü\

do do do do

Do not enter.

for

\fər, (ˈ)fȯr, Southern also (ˈ)fär\

for for for for

This is for charity.

go

\ˈgō\

go go go go

She wants to go now.

has

\'has, (h)əs\

has has has has

Your father has a sister.

have

\ˈhav, (h)əv\

have have have have

I have no money.

he

\ˈhē, ē\

he he he he

He is William.

here

\'hir\

here here here here

They do not belong here.

\ˈin, ən\

in in in in

Let's get in!

is

\'iz, 'is\

is is is is

She is dancing.

\ˈit, ət\

it it it it

It was an accident.

like

\ˈlīk\

like like like like

She likes to play games.

look

\ˈlu̇k\

look look look look

She looks like a doll.

me

\ˈmē\

me me me me

Please give me that!

my

\ˈmī, mə\

my my my my

He is my cousin.

no

\ˈnō\

no no no no

She had no socks.

play

\ˈplā\

play play play play

She plays the drum.

said

\ˈsed\

said said said said

She said yes.

see

\ˈsē\

see see see see

You should see a doctor.

she

\ˈshē\

she she she she

She is beautiful.

the

\thə, ˈthē\

the the the the

The sky is blue.

to

\tə, tu̇, ˈtü\

to to to to

She was married to him.

up

\ˈəp\

up up up up

She is up there.

we

\ˈwē\

we we we we

We have to go now.

Visit
BABY PROFESSOR
EDUCATION KIDS
www.BabyProfessorBooks.com
to download Free Baby Professor eBooks
and view our catalog of new and exciting
Children's Books

www.ingramcontent.com/pod-product-compliance
Lightning Source LLC
LaVergne TN
LVHW082307150826
845677LV00009B/1744

* 9 7 9 8 8 6 9 4 4 9 6 6 5 *